My Visits to Heaven

– Lessons Learned –

Matthew Robert Payne

To sow into Matthew's writing ministry, to request a personal prophecy or life coaching or to contact him, please visit http://personal-prophecy-today.com.

Cover designed by akira007 at fiverr.com.

Unless otherwise indicated, all Scripture is taken from the New King James Version. Copyright © 1982 by Thomas Nelson, Inc. Used by permission. All rights reserved.

New Living Translation (NLT). Holy Bible, New Living Translation, copyright © 1996, 2004, 2015 by Tyndale House Foundation. Used by permission of Tyndale House Publishers Inc., Carol Stream, Illinois 60188. All rights reserved.

The opinions expressed by the author are not necessarily those of Revival Waves of Glory Books & Publishing.

Published by Revival Waves of Glory Books & Publishing PO Box 596| Litchfield, Illinois 62056 USA

www.revivalwavesofgloryministries.com.

Revival Waves of Glory Books & Publishing is committed to excellence in the publishing industry. Book design Copyright © 2017 by Revival Waves of Glory Books & Publishing. All rights reserved.

Paperback: 978-1-365-81195-1

Hardcover: 978-1-365-81199-9

Table of Contents

Dedications

The book is dedicated to the Holy Spirit who led me to Jesus, led me to meet the Father, provided communication between the Father and Jesus with me, and who has inspired and co-authored all my books.

This book is also dedicated to my angels that have been with me and assisted me in all that I do on this earth.

This book is also dedicated to all the hungry people in the world that want to experience heaven before they die.

Acknowledgements

To the unnamed sponsor of this book

A heartfelt thank you goes out to the sponsor of this book who felt impressed by the Holy Spirit to fully fund the related production costs. This anonymous individual took it upon himself to ask if he could sponsor the cost of editing, cover design and the publishing of this book. It is my prayer that many people read this book and that they are blessed by his generous donation. If you would like to sponsor one of my books, please email me and ask me how you can help.

Father God

I want to thank you for loving me, for leading me and for making me into the person that I am today. Thank you for your Son, my best friend.

Jesus Christ

Thank you for being my friend for all of my life. You have led me and trained me, and you have allowed me to write some encouraging books. You are a joy to me. You introduced me to your Father, and now, I am getting to know him better through the years. You are closer to me than any other person outside my mother.

Bill Vincent

I want to thank Bill Vincent, who produces my paperback books, my e-books and my audio books. His company, Revival Waves of Glory Books & Publishing, has shown me great favor, and without you, I would be spending a lot more money to produce books. I give you my heartfelt thanks.

The Readers

I want to thank my readers. You have motivated me to write this. I hope that you really enjoy it and that you manage to have your own visit to heaven in the coming years. Don't be afraid to let me help you with that.

June and Bob Payne

I want to thank my mother and father for inviting me home for my annual holidays and for giving me a wonderful home with three cooked meals each day and a relaxing atmosphere so that I could edit this book. Everyone needs to have people in their life that love them for who they are and not for what they can do for them.

Introduction

If you are anything like me, one of your favorite subjects is heaven. It is so hard to find a really good book on heaven. The best book that I have read on the subject is "Revealing Heaven" by Kat Kerr. I don't feel that my book is as well-written as hers, but if you love heaven, it is my prayer that this short book of mine will not only inspire you to go to there but that you might even visit while you read it.

Heaven is a place of our inheritance through Christ's shed blood. The Bible says that we are already seated in heavenly places. If you can imagine yourself seated next to Jesus on a throne, then all you really need to do is open your spiritual eyes, and you will be in heaven.

During the course of this book, I hope to encourage you about heaven and to teach you the qualities that you might need to visit there and to share with you the lessons that I learned from my encounters. It is my prayer that you will add this book to your catalogue of books on heaven and that one day, before you die, you experience visits for yourself. I have included exercises in this book that, if approached with faith, might even help you encounter heaven before you finish reading it. If you do not have an encounter in heaven by reading this book, you can contact me via my website for more information on how you can access your own trip there.

Enjoy!

Chapter 1

Trip to the Throne Room — Part 1

I was once at a church and went forward for prophetic ministry. I connected with a prayer partner who also happened to be gifted in counseling. This person stated, "When I pray, you will see something in your mind. I want you to tell me what you see."

As he prayed for me, I immediately found myself in a vision of heaven with Jesus standing in front of me. The prayer partner asked, "What do you see?"

I responded, "I'm in heaven."

He was shocked. "Okay. What can you see?"

I answered, "Jesus is standing in front of me."

"What is Jesus doing, or what he is saying?"

I replied, "Jesus is taking off his robe, and he's putting it on me."

The counselor continued, "What is he doing now?"

"He is taking off his crown, and he's giving it to me."

I was a little overcome, and the counselor questioned, "What's he doing now?"

I reported, "He's taking off his signet ring, and he's putting it onto my finger."

The prayer partner told me that Jesus was showing me that I have authority in the Kingdom as signified by the signet ring.

"What is Jesus is doing now?"

I indicated, "Jesus is asking me to come into the throne room to meet his Father."

The prayer partner queried, "So, are you going?"

I replied, "No," and I started to cry.

The prayer partner wondered, "Why are you crying?"

I admitted, "I'm not worthy."

The prayer partner gently corrected me. "Jesus died for the forgiveness of your sins, and Jesus' blood made you worthy to enter the throne room, so you can go in."

I confessed, "I'm scared."

The counselor continued, "Jesus is holding your hand. There's nothing to be scared of."

With that, I went through these double doors, the entrance to the throne room. As I entered from the back, thousands of people were in the room. These people seemed to part to make an aisle for me and for Jesus to walk up. I was walking down the aisle toward his throne, which you could see in the distance.

As I walked toward the throne, I fell over eight times and eight times, Jesus lifted me to my feet. I learned later that eight is a number of new beginnings. I arrived at the front at an elevated spot in front of the throne. I saw about 100 stairs up to the actual thrones, and Jesus left me there. I heard the Father say, "Come up here, Matthew." I went up the stairs, and the Father told me to sit down on Jesus' throne.

Later, after this vision, I checked and found this verse in Revelation 3:21 where Jesus says, "To him who overcomes I will grant to sit with Me on My throne, as I also overcame and sat down with My Father on His throne."

Theologically speaking, I was permitted to be in the throne room and to be sitting on Jesus' throne. The Father looked at me, and he said, "Have a look at this." The roof of heaven seemed to blow off the throne room, and you could see up into the galaxy.

Planets and stars seemed as if they were 1,000 to 2,000 miles from heaven. The celestial bodies were very close, and if it were like earth with gravity, they would have crashed down on top of us. But these planets or stars hung suspended in space, and gravity did not affect them.

Anyway, this view of the galaxies was the best view I'd ever seen in my life. The Father asked me, "Can you see all of those stars? Can you see that galaxy?"

I answered, "Yeah."

God stated, "I control all of that. If I sent one of those stars down to earth, that would be the end of your planet."

I agreed, "Yes, it would be."

The Father asked, "Don't you think if I can control all of that, that I can control your life?"

My eyes filled with tears as I told the prayer minister what the Father said. The prayer minister was repeating everything that I was saying. I was glad in a way because the two-part process of hearing and then repeating what he said allowed me to remember this vision very clearly.

I've read a book from an Indian apostle who has been to heaven. He was also seated on Jesus' throne, and the Father opened up the galaxies and showed him the same exact scene and repeated the same exact words. "Don't you think if I can control all of this, I can control your life?"

I was very interested to find out years later that the exact same occurrence and exact same vision happened to this Indian apostle. I've read a lot of books on heaven, and some of my experiences in heaven are the same as those of other authors. Other writers tell about their similar visits to heaven. I was very interested in hearing that this apostle had been to heaven and experienced exactly the same vision with exactly the same words from God the Father. God must repeat himself to several of us.

Lessons Learned

I found it very interesting that Jesus met me and led me into the throne room. John 14:6 tells us that the only way to the Father is through Jesus. Jesus provided the welcome to heaven; he gave me his robe of righteousness and his crown for overcoming and "dressed me" to appear before his Father.

It is exciting to know that the very first vision that I had of heaven was a visit to meet God. Today, over 10 years later, I am still overcome with my visit to meet God in his throne room. I was excited that I could actually meet God and even more excited to learn that God wanted to take control of my life.

God would love to lead everyone's life, and it should not take a trip to heaven for you to submit your life to his leading.

Provision has been made through the shed blood of Jesus for any believer to be welcomed into heaven. I hope that you are encouraged and that you want to go to heaven as you read this book.

Chapter 2

Trip to the Throne Room — Part 2

Two weeks before this vision, I was on the toilet listening to a worship song by Delirious with the chorus that repeats, "I could sing of your love forever; I could sing of your love forever" numerous times.

I had a sexual addiction and regularly visited prostitutes. It's important to share about my addiction with you in this book so that you know that I have my own struggles and temptations just like everyone else. As the song was playing those words, I started to sing it to Jesus.

As the song progressed, the next time I came to the chorus, I heard the voice change on the recording on the stereo. I now heard Jesus' voice actually singing the song, "I could sing of your love forever."

I just started to cry because I had just slept with a prostitute four days before this, and Jesus was singing to me, "I could sing of your love forever." His love for me really touched me deeply. I asked him, "Are you singing this song to me?"

He answered, "Not only that, but in the future, I'm going to sing this song to the whole of heaven and dedicate it to you."

When Father asked, "Won't you let me control your life?" I was thinking about this addiction to prostitutes. I was so overcome that I was in the throne room talking to God, and here I was, a person addicted to prostitutes.

This was the reason why I was afraid of meeting God when I was outside with Jesus. I thought that I was such a sinner that I was going to be struck dead for my sin in the presence of God the Father.

So here I was, seated on the throne, and Jesus came. It was like he grabbed a microphone and announced, "I'm going to dedicate this song to Matthew." The music started, and Jesus started to sing, "Over the mountains and the sea, your river runs with love for me...." and the song goes on. I was listening to the first verse, and then, he started to sing, "I could sing of your love forever," in the chorus.

He was singing it to the congregation of thousands of people in the throne room. I was in tears because Jesus, two weeks after this conversation on the toilet, long before I had left my addiction to prostitutes, was singing this song about me, saying that he could sing of my love forever. He was really demonstrating grace. Some people might read this book thus far and heard my testimony. My transparency and this much vulnerability stopped you from reading, and for whatever reason, you judged me. You thought, "It's not possible to go to heaven and certainly not possible for a sinner like Matthew to go to heaven."

So, if you need to stop reading, go ahead and stop reading.

Jesus sang that song to me, and I was overcome, I didn't realize two weeks before, when I was sitting on the toilet, that

Jesus would sing that song to me so soon. I thought that was going to happen at the end of my life.

It was my first visit to heaven; so, it was amazing.

After Jesus finished the song, he gave the floor to some of the saints of the Bible, who followed in a procession—Paul, David, Noah, Moses and Abraham. Each of them came up and stood in front of the throne where I was seated. At the bottom of the throne, down the hundred stairs and in front of the congregation of worshippers, they stood and waved to me, and I'd sense the name of the saint in my head, for example, Abraham. He'd walk away. The next person would come along, and I'd hear their name in my spirit—Moses. Moses would wave and then walk away.

A procession of saints from the Bible came, and once I heard their name, they'd wave at me, and then they would walk off.

At the end of the procession, Joseph was standing there with the coat of many colors. He didn't leave but just waited. The prayer minister asked me, "What color is the robe that Jesus gave you?"

I replied, "It was white."

The prayer minister instructed, "Now, I want you to look down right now and tell me what color the robe is." I looked down, and it was a coat of many colors. I was wearing the coat of Joseph that his father, Jacob, had given him.

I was told by Jesus that this was my mantle and that Joseph had imparted his mantle to me, which was very precious. That was the end of my first visit to heaven.

I've read many books from people about heaven, and I've read books about the throne room and people visiting there. Many people describe the throne as high and lifted up, and I would estimate that there are 50 to 100 stairs between the bottom of the platform and where God's throne resides at the top.

When I saw God, I saw him as a ball of light. I didn't see him as a man. I saw Jesus as a man and the saints as men.

In the actual throne room, I saw thousands of people. I didn't see millions of people. I saw a crowd of possibly 10,000 people. I didn't realize that there was a roof to the throne room. When the Father opened up the roof and I saw the galaxy, I could see through the roof of the throne room. I don't know if the galaxy is always there, and I worshipped under the stars or if there's an extra roof that came over the throne room as I've imagined that there would be.

In the throne room, I didn't see 24 elders. I didn't see the four living creatures. I didn't see a rainbow coming out of the throne. I didn't see lightning. All I saw was God as a ball of light, sitting on the throne.

I saw Jesus down below, singing. Jesus never came up to the throne. He left me at the bottom while I went up to meet the Father. Then, he was singing on what looked like a microphone, but that's probably just my perception from earth.

Apparently, we take our perceptions from earth into heaven along with our own theologies, and we see things differently in heaven according to what we already believe and according to lenses that we wear on our consciousness.

Different people can approach and see things in the throne room, but they see through a lens of their theology, and I'm thinking that affects what they actually see.

That's an encouraging story for the first chapter of the book, and I will share more of my experiences as I continue.

Lessons Learned

When I first went to heaven, I had been called as a prophet but was not in the office of prophet. I learned that because of the shed innocent blood of Jesus, our sins are forgiven, and therefore, we can come boldly to the throne of grace. We need to remember that we don't need to be perfect or in a sinless state to meet God. You'll remember that God told me that he wanted to take control of my life. Part of him taking control was allowing me the grace to walk free from my addiction years later.

Many people might read this book and be disturbed that a man addicted to prostitutes was allowed into heaven. The might think that this was totally unscriptural, but I don't see it as such. Instead, I see this experience as a testament to the mighty grace and love of the Lord Jesus and his Father. If we all had to be sinless before we went to heaven, some of us would never be able to have an encounter.

Many of us see ourselves as unholy, unrighteous and dirty, which sadly stops us from intimately encountering God. Jesus, despite my sad addiction, felt led to sing to all of heaven and boast of my love for him. We really do not see ourselves the way God sees us through the righteousness of Christ.

Another lesson that we can learn from this encounter is that we do not need to go to the outer edges of heaven before we enter the throne room. When God wanted to bring me to heaven, he had me come directly to see him. How great is the

Father that he would bring me to his throne on my first visit. God knew what effect this visit would have on me.

We can also see from this visit that Jesus not only wanted to honor me and sing a song about his love for me to the people and angels in the throne room, but he also wanted to introduce me to the great patriarchs of the faith. Meeting these saints in heaven was the first time I met a saint from the Bible, but it was soon to be a common experience in my life.

Chapter 3

Vision of the Great Wall

Once, I had a vision of heaven while I was on earth. In my vision, I was taken to heaven where I saw this great wall. I was in front of this great wall with all this mist. At the time, I didn't know what to call the mist. I didn't know about glory clouds then, so I didn't have a word in my vocabulary for what I was seeing. I saw this wall that rose up about 100 feet into this mist. The wall stretched beyond where the mist started, but you could not see how high the wall went.

The wall looked like it could be hundreds of feet high and possibly miles long. I remember sharing the vision when I first saw it years ago. Someone told me, "It could very well be the wall of the New Jerusalem that's mentioned in the Bible." The wall measures 144 cubits (Revelation 21:17).

As I was looking at this wall, I heard Jesus say, "Reach into the wall." I put my hand in into the wall and pulled out a precious stone the size of soccer ball.

Jesus told me in my spirit, "The stone that you're holding in your hand is a diamond." This made sense to me because the Bible has descriptions of precious stones.

The wall was completely made from these diamonds. Then, I heard Jesus say, "The diamond in your hand could run the finances of the U.S. government for 200 years." I was surprised and really shocked by that statement.

As I write this, I've spent the last two years watching the American presidential race with Donald Trump. I've heard figures and budgets and numbers related to the American economy. This makes the worth of the diamond so much more than what I initially realized when I was told by Jesus that the diamond could run the U.S. government expenditure for 200 years.

Jesus told me, "Now, this whole wall is made of diamonds like that." That statement had a profound effect. I was thinking about what an amazing amount of money that was if just one of those diamonds in that wall could run the U.S. government for so long. The worth of the wall, which was hundreds of feet high and even miles long, would be astounding!

I didn't know exactly how long or how high the wall was because of the glory cloud blocking my vision so that I could not see the length or the height of the wall.

I was stunned with the amount of money this represented! As I was considering the worth of the whole wall, God the Father announced, "That's what we think of money up here, Matthew."

I've shared this story with quite a few people and now, I'm sharing it with you. It really had a profound effect on me. Those words sunk in, and I think the vision I had and the real purpose of it was that God was showing me that money was meaningless in heaven.

What earth considers as two century's worth of government spending was just one diamond in my hand, and tens of thousands of those diamonds were in that wall. The amount comes to an almost incomprehensible figure.

I had that vision many years ago, and I heard God say, "That's what money means to us up here." I've been in ministry for a few years and have had people donate to me. Just recently, in the last month, two people asked me how much it is to finance one of my books, and I told them $1,500 Australian. They both financed books, including this one, and gave me the money to pay for them.

What I've realized from God's statement is that God can move on the hearts of people to give you money. God can move on the hearts of others to prosper you. What is of real worth in heaven is someone with a pure heart, someone with a heart that's sold out, someone with a heart that doesn't consider the wealth and the possessions and the things of this world.

When you've got a heart that's sold out for God, when you've got a precious heart that only wants God's ways and God's desires and only wants to do what God wants you to do, you please God. That's when God can open up the blessings of heaven and pour out his finances on you and supply your needs.

To do great things, God only has to bring one of those diamonds to earth or even a little diamond to earth. People already have gem stones appearing in their houses. God only has to bring one of these faultless diamonds to earth and give it to you. If you sell it, you could easily pay the mortgage on your house.

God reinforced to me that money isn't important to heaven. Other matters are more important than money to God. He treasures a pure, contrite and humble heart above any sort of finances.

I can't be sold on wealth, and that's why my books are 99 cents, the cheapest they're allowed to be on Amazon. I can't be bought by money or cajoled by money or motivated or moved or controlled by people trying to bring money to me. I can only be controlled by the will of God.

Lessons Learned

The world we live in is controlled by people who have power through wealth. Many people consider possessing a lot of money as a sign of God's blessing in your life. The lesson I learned from that encounter is that money has relatively little meaning to God. Sure, money can be used to do great things, but God does not seem to place much importance on it. That is why he has a wall in heaven made of priceless gems.

However, God loves a person who draws close to him and lives to do his will. God admires people who lay down their whole lives and their personal ambitions in order to serve God. He can powerfully use people that are wholly dedicated to him when it comes to Kingdom finances. I admire people like Joseph Prince, Joyce Meyer and Andrew Wommack who have many millions of dollars that flow through their ministries. They live a life that is holy and wholly pleasing to God.

Jesus asked on earth, "What is the use of inheriting the whole world and losing your own soul?" I was forever touched by this vision; it showed me that money is not important in the scheme of things. I hope that you come to the same conclusion from this story.

Chapter 4

Visiting Children in Heaven

One thing I want to share with you before I go into further details about this story is that in the early stages of my visits to heaven, God was in control. As I went about my business on earth as a regular person, busy with activities, all of a sudden, I ended up on a visitation to heaven.

I didn't pursue it. It wasn't something I was seeking or desiring. I was just living my Christian life, and all of a sudden, I'd end up in heaven. I have now reached a stage in my Christian life where I can choose to go to heaven anytime I like, but that wasn't always the case.

I always visit heaven in my mind. I'm not there physically. I see things through my mind, and that's how I visit heaven.

Some people actually see their spirits leave their body, and they see their body on the ground. They go up through the atmosphere and end up in heaven. I don't go to heaven like that. I see heaven in my mind, and I can be on earth, looking at things on earth and then the next minute, I'll be seeing pictures and images in my mind, and I'm in heaven.

One day, I was going about my business, and suddenly, I found myself at the edge of this park where hundreds and hundreds of children were playing. They were wrestling, jumping rope and playing on this playground equipment. One of the rides spun around like a carousel, round, round and round. You push it, and then you jump on it, and you go around on this ride that's like a carousel.

All of these children were playing, and I looked around, but no adults were watching them. I grew concerned, and I heard Jesus say in my spirit, "No pedophiles are here, Matthew. It makes a lot of sense for the children not to have adult supervision because when the children are just alone, they take more risks and have a lot more fun than when adults are watching."

I agreed, "Yeah, that's true, that's really true." I watched the children wrestling on the ground and skipping rope, and they were having a lot of fun.

I saw a girl sitting on a bench, and she looked at me and then walked up to me. She greeted me, "Hello, Matthew."

I asked, "You know my name?"

She replied, "Yes, I know you." It was really amazing. She added, "I know your son."

At that time, I hadn't seen my son in years because of the breakdown in my marriage.

I asked, "How do you know my son?"

She replied, "I talked to him and played with him in his dreams. I told him about how your life is going and showed him pictures about how you're doing." Her words made me cry. I missed my son so much. Heaven seems to do that to you; it fills you with tears.

She said that she keeps in contact with my son and that she is his friend. My son dreams about her and plays with her in heaven.

I was really emotional. She questioned, "Do you want to see my favorite place?"

I said, "Yeah," and she grabbed my hand, which is a type of communication device in heaven and in spiritual matters. Clairvoyants and psychics understand this concept and will grab hands and do meditations and similar activities while holding hands. However, the impartation of touch through holding hands was birthed from God with spiritual implications, so that is why many of us hold hands when we say grace before a meal.

She took hold of my hand. As soon as she grabbed my hand, we were in this meadow and grassland. A fence was running up the hill for about a mile. She queried, "Can you look down there in the bottom corner?" I looked down and saw some buildings. She told me, "They are the stables."

I responded, "Stables for what?"

She replied, "They're for the horses of heaven. Here come some now." A couple of horses galloped up to the fence, and she went forward and touched the horses and patted them.

She indicated, "These are the horses of heaven. This is where I come to ride."

I asked, "Do you ride these horses?"

She replied, "Yes, I ride these horses. I love to ride the horses in heaven."

I wondered, "Have you ever ridden with Michael, the Archangel?"

She reported, "Yes, I have. He has a special horse that he rides, and I've been on his horse." I was totally amazed.

The girl was about 14 years of age. You can bet any girl around that age would love to ride horses. God is so good.

Here is some information for you. That whole park was full of children who had been aborted by their mothers on earth. For these children, that park is a place for them to play and have fun.

Each of those children has foster parents in heaven. Parents in their 20s and 30s bring them up and raise them. They've got grandfathers and grandparents in heaven. People up in heaven who are older and more mature look after them and mentor them and act as parents and grandparents to them.

If you die before you're 8 to 10 on earth, you immediately go to heaven. You're counted as an innocent, and all these children are waiting for their mothers to make a decision for Christ. They're all hoping that their mothers will become Christians and come to heaven.

These children are happy. They're playing in this park. They've got a school in heaven. They are taught the Bible in heaven in Bible school. They are taught reading and writing and arithmetic and philosophy and religion and all sorts of interesting information, and they have a really rich life.

I've visited the children many times in heaven. For a few years, the children were sort of counseling me and being my friends because I had a lot of hurt and pain in my life.

Lessons Learned

What lesson did I learn from this visitation? First of all, I learned that even though I was separated from my son for many years, God was still working in my son's life. I learned that children can go to heaven in their dreams. It makes sense that adults can also go to heaven in their dreams.

I think it is important for people to know that every miscarriage, every stillborn baby, every child that dies under the age of 10 and every child that is aborted ends up living and growing up in heaven. If you know someone that has had an abortion, they would be really blessed to read this book.

Often, I have spoken to mothers who have lost a child through various means, and I have been able to bring them a message from their child. Many mothers who have had miscarriages have no idea of the gender of that child, so they can't name their baby. Through the help of the Holy Spirit, I am able to have a vision of their child and bring them a message of hope.

I have been to heaven many times and visited these children, and all of these children would love to know their earthly parents. It is my hope that, through a book like this, people might not only come to know their children are alive, but they might also grow in faith to a point where they can visit their children in heaven.

Chapter 5

Waltzing with Jesus

I have to say that a beneficial way to progress in the Kingdom is to be obedient and to be a person who's submitted to God.

Obedience plays a major role in the life of a Christian who wants to have an intimate relationship with Jesus. I wrote a book called "7 Keys to Intimacy with Jesus," and one of the seven keys that I've mentioned and explained was obedience.

Jesus says in John 14:15, "If you love me, obey my commandments." He actually says that four times in the gospel of John. "If you love me, obey my commandments." Jesus is really into obedience. I think that if you're obedient, have childlike faith and if you're teachable, you can do great things.

"Those who accept my commandments and obey them are the ones who love me. And because they love me, my Father will love them. And I will love them and reveal myself to each of them" John 14:21 (New Living Translation).

Being teachable means being open for new lines of thought, new understandings and new teachings. If you're teachable, you'll sometimes find that you're actually wrong about what you believe and that the truth is completely opposite of what you thought was correct. What used to annoy you when some people preached on a certain subject was actually the Holy Spirit tugging on you to go that way.

When you're teachable, you'll be turned around eventually, and you'll be enlightened to the truth. These are some keys to having encounters with God.

But let's focus on obedience. I was at church one day and saw a good example of it. The church was really free and had praise and worship, and they had a real freedom in their worship. They allowed people to dance with flags and wave their banners. They allowed people to do prophetic and spiritual dancing at the front. They allowed all sorts of activities that promoted freedom and really had beautiful pastors that were open to the Holy Spirit.

I was standing worshiping and singing the songs, and because I can hear Jesus speak to me, Jesus said to me, "I want you to waltz with me."

I asked, "Here?"

Jesus replied, "Yeah. I want you to go out and put your hands out and imagine me dancing with you, and I want you to waltz with me." I agreed, so I went out, and I wouldn't have done that in a normal church, but this church allowed worship with freedom. I put my hand out behind Jesus' back, and he appeared in a vision in my hands. I could feel and see Jesus embracing me, and we started to waltz. Here I was, waltzing with Jesus at the front of this church to the worship music.

Well, I was only waltzing for about a minute, and then, we disappeared from the church and appeared at the base of the stairs in the throne room between the audience and God's throne. God was on his throne, and Jesus and I appeared in the throne room, waltzing in front of all the worshippers.

That was just an absolutely amazing experience. Many people have heard of the Wedding Supper of the Lamb. At the Wedding Supper of the Lamb, Jesus actually has the wedding with his Bride. He establishes the actual nuptials, the actual ceremony of marrying his Bride.

Heaven is not limited by time, so one day in heaven is like two weeks of time on earth. Since there's plenty of time in heaven, everyone who's saved and everyone who's a Christian at the Wedding Supper of the Lamb will have a chance to waltz and dance with Jesus. All of you women who are reading this or listening to this as an audio book might really desire to dance with Jesus at the Wedding Supper of the Lamb. Everyone who wants to dance with Jesus will dance with him.

So, here I was, waltzing with Jesus in front of the congregation of heaven. At that time, I'd had already had the revelation that everyone was going to dance with Jesus in the Wedding Supper of the Lamb.

This vision meant so much to me. It was so glorious to be in the throne room. There's a real energy. There's a real buzz in this throne room. It's the most anointed place that you could be, and it was really exciting to be in front of thousands of people, dancing with the King of Kings. I don't have the ability to perform an amazing waltz. I have just enough skill to pass so that I could actually dance for about a minute before everyone else joins at the real wedding if I do get married in the future.

A loose paraphrase of the Scripture verse in Psalms 84:10 says, "One day in your court is worth a thousand elsewhere." Waltzing with Jesus in the throne room is an amazing and profound experience. Even as I write and share about this, it deeply affects me to remember that encounter.

Some might say, "Well, that just happened in your imagination." On the other hand, you can replay memories of traumatic events in your imagination, and the actual events as you thought about them really disturb you and cause all sorts of negative emotions. The same is true when I replay this event that happened in my imagination; it really brings up amazing and profound love and expectation in me. It is really a fond memory to have.

Lessons Learned

This is another lesson about obedience and the rewards that come from it. It was just another evening at a church. I had no idea that I would be caught up to heaven. Jesus simply told me to waltz and next thing I knew, I was in heaven.

Every time Jesus tells you to do something, he has a reason behind it. Jesus is wise and profound, and even if we can't see why he told us to do something right away, he always has a reason.

This experience was one of my fondest memories. I have learned to obey Jesus every time he tells me to do something. Who knows, the next time you are told to do something, Jesus might really surprise you.

Some might ask the purpose of this vision. That is a good question. I would like to say that when you are friends with Jesus, he doesn't need a reason to pour out his love and surprises on you. I really do find that one day in God's courts is better than a thousand elsewhere as it says in Psalms 84.

Chapter 6

Worshipping with Jesus

In the last chapter, I spent some time saying that one of the keys to visitations and the ability to see heaven and encounter angels and the supernatural is to have childlike faith, a faith that is willing to explore. Even the Bereans knew that they should listen intently to what Paul had to say, and then they searched the Scriptures to see that it was true. However, they listened excitedly to what Paul had to say and then went and checked faithfully to ensure that Paul's words lined up with what was written.

Childlike faith is amazing, and obedience is another real integral key to a successful life with Jesus. He had many things to teach us.

Jesus really enjoys it when we obey him, and true acts of obedience develop our faith. It's almost as if obedience acts as an entrance gate, as a gateway to the supernatural.

I'm endeavoring to give you some teaching as I share these encounters with you so that you have some keys and insights into how to have these sorts of experiences for yourself.

I want to share another love story of obedience. I was at church one day, listening to a song. The lyrics went something like this, "And I will get down on my knees, and I'll worship you." Some songs actually mention that you should kneel down and worship.

As the song played the first time, I think during the chorus, I felt the Holy Spirit nudge me. "You might as well sing this song on your knees." When we sang the second chorus, Jesus actually said to me, "Matthew, I want you to get on your knees and sing this to me." Jesus spoke to me the second time, even though the song was addressed to God, the Father. It wasn't addressed to Jesus.

I got down on my knees, and something happened that I wasn't expecting. As I raised my hands to worship, Jesus appeared in a vision and got on his knees and raised his hands in worship. Here I was with Jesus on the floor in the front of my church, worshipping God, and it was such an amazing feeling to be on my knees, worshipping God with Jesus next to me.

I'm not sure many of you have encountered Jesus like that while worshipping, but it really is a powerful experience.

So, here I was on my knees, worshipping Jesus, and we worshipped for about 20 seconds. After 20 seconds, we left the church, and we appeared in the throne room. Once again, we were at the base of the 100 stairs, and God was up on his throne, shining like a ball of light.

Jesus and I were in front of the 10,000 people standing and worshipping. Both Jesus and I were on our knees with our arms extended, worshipping his Father. I have to tell you that while it was wonderful to dance and waltz with Jesus in front of the Father, it was just another totally amazing and jaw-dropping experience to see the Son of God, to see Jesus Christ, the King of Kings, on his knees in submission, worshipping the Father in the throne room.

The whole throne room was singing the song that was playing on earth. The whole throne room was singing the same song that my church was singing, and Jesus and I had our arms raised and were worshipping the Father, and it was glorious. It was an amazing encounter.

Once again, I have to say that I agree with the words of David that one day in the courts of heaven is better than a thousand elsewhere. I've often thought of that encounter, which lasted for about two minutes, and I've often thought that those two minutes were worth 2,000 hours elsewhere.

Certainly, I wouldn't trade that vision or that encounter that I had for five years of living. It was just breathtaking. It was absolutely mind boggling to encounter Jesus worshipping his Father and to be right next to him on my knees, a partner in worship with him together.

It's amazing thing to be in a congregation of saints, watching Jesus on his knees, worshipping his Father in front of you. That scene would really affect you. But to be partners with him, almost holding his hand as he worshipped his Father and to be seated right next to him and hear him singing with his whole heart and with his voice raised to his Father in heaven was something else.

Through this tremendous encounter, I actually saw that Jesus is not only obedient, subservient and acknowledging of his Father, he is under his Father's authority. I also saw Jesus on his knees, worshipping his Father in the throne room in front of the courts and the congregation of heaven. This was an amazing and life-changing experience for me.

I hope that as you read this or listen to it on Audible that you can see the 10,000 people standing up in line. I hope that you can see a space between that and the 100 stairs up to the throne. In the space between the stairs and the people, I hope you can see Jesus and me on our knees with our hands raised high, worshipping the Father.

I hope you can see that vision. You might even put on some worship music and step into that vision and come on in and experience it with us. As you play your music, listen and see if the throne room starts to play that same music and see if you're actually kneeling down beside Jesus and praising the Father. Maybe you'll start to have your own encounter.

Lesson Learned

You might know that Jesus is God's Son in your mind, but to encounter Jesus in a subservient way on his knees worshipping his Father is something else entirely.

Do you know that Jesus not only loves his Father but worships him also? Do you know that Jesus, who has ascended so that his name is above all names, still is a servant to his Father?

In this experience, I was totally astounded. I was not only encouraged that I could take part in it, but I was overcome with love for Jesus and his Father. I hope that as you read the encounter that I had, that you can get a picture of it and somehow have a similar experience so that you can understand what happened.

I always knew that Jesus paid honor to his Father, but I learned in a most holy way that Jesus holds his Father in high esteem and will worship him in humility. I am overcome at the memory of this vision.

I hope that you can put on some worship music, get on your knees and worship God. Have Jesus join you and the both of you can go to heaven and worship his Father together also.

Chapter 7

Taking a Friend to Heaven

(An encounter and an exercise for you as well.)

As you read this encounter, see if you can engage with it in your imagination. I had a friend that I knew fairly well. When I first met this friend, I sensed the presence of the Lord on him, and he seemed to really stand out. I was staying at a homeless men's hostel at that time. I was going through a hard time with my mental illness.

I was experiencing hardship, and I was staying at this hostel that slept about 150 men. About 500 men used to visit the hostel for meals. One day, I was having a meal, and I saw this guy walk in, and I noticed a presence on him. I've noticed a spiritual presence on warlocks and witches before, but I'd never encountered such a presence on anyone before I met this person.

I found that this person was a Christian and a person who had outright different views from me about certain things. However, he had a love for Jesus. I was friends with him around Easter, and he experienced stigmata at that time where his hands became very painful. He was a very spiritual person.

I was talking with him once, and the subject of heaven came up. It was the first time that I've ever done this before with a person. I grabbed his hand, and I told him, "Imagine this. You can go to heaven with me right now." Dear reader, you can do this with me as you read this book. See if it happens to you, too.

Now, pretend that I'm grabbing your hand as you keep reading. I told him, "See a fountain in your mind with three levels. It has one level, then the second level, then the third level. It's round, white and made of marble with nice parts on it that look as if they are crusted. The fountain is blowing water from the top that is dripping down from the top to the middle to the bottom. In the bottom of the fountain, a white lion is actually walking around with a lamb."

"Right now, as you're looking at the fountain, the lion is swishing his tail and looking at you. Can you see the lion looking at you?"

He answered, "Yes."

I told him, "The lion is walking toward you, and if you put out your hand, he'll lick it."

He held out his hand, and the lion licked his hand.

I went on. "So, you have encountered the lion. Behind the fountain, there are about 30 children."

He nodded.

I asked, "Can you see them?"

He replied, "Yeah."

I continued, "One of the children, a young boy, is walking around the fountain and coming up to you. He has something in his hands. What has he got in his hands?"

If you're reading this, what does the boy have in his hands? What does the boy have for you, and what color is his skin? Is he a white boy, or is he black, or is he Asian? Answer the question for yourself. You can write to me and tell me your response.

"The boy has a small box in his hand."

I asked, "What's inside the box?"

He opened the box, which contained a ring. "It has a ring in it."

I answered, "You can take the ring out of the box and put it on your finger."

He took the ring out of the box and put it on his finger.

I went on. "Okay. The boy will hold your hand and take you with him." My friend took the boy's hand, and I said, "He's taking you around the other side of the fountain. A path is there that's made of gold. The path rises up the hill, so walk up the path with him."

I explained, "As you come to the crest of the hill, you can see a city in the distance. You can see all the glory. It's shining."

He nodded. "Yeah, I can see that."

"The boy is holding your hand now. He's going to take you to a park." He went to a park, the same park that we talked about in chapter 4. The park was full of hundreds of children playing and going on rides. A child in the park interacted with him, talking with him, asking questions and telling him about a number of things.

I realized that all I had to do was to hold a person's hand and introduce him to the fountain with the children. If you are reading this book, you might have seen the fountain and the lion walking around, swishing his tail as I described it. You might have seen the lion looking at you while you held the hand of a little boy or a little girl, depending on your gender. A little girl might hand you a pen, a sword, a Bible or a book. Each person will likely see a different gift, depending on who they are. If you hold the child's hand, you can go walking in the park and see the city of heaven in the future. You can spend time interacting with the other children in the park.

As I've taken many people to heaven, a portal has opened with potential to just introduce people to heaven. This portal actually exists in heaven. It's an actual place in heaven, a place of contact that I have so that I can introduce people to heaven.

I have taken about 20 people to that portal and to heaven, and different people at different times have gone from there to the park with the children. Then, I have taken them from the park with the children into the throne room.

What I'm describing is a portal in heaven, and I hope as you read this, you put on some worship music. Perhaps you can pray and read it again and imagine it as you go with the children. If you want to visit certain places in heaven, just ask the child to take you to those places and hold the child's hand. The child will appear at the places that you want to go.

Lessons Learned

This was the first time I took a person to heaven. I was led and guided by the Holy Spirit who must have opened up the portal/access point to heaven. Since then, I have taken about 20 people to heaven, as I have already said. I take many people to heaven via Skype. You can contact me via my website, and we can try and take you to heaven also.

Jesus would love more people to come to heaven. As you experience Jesus and experience heaven, life can become more bearable and exciting for you. I serve a God who has us positionally seated in heavenly places as Christians, and going to heaven is us simply exercising our rights.

The day I took my friend to heaven, he was down and a bit depressed. We were talking about heaven, and I heard that Bob Jones held people's hands and took them to heaven. I thought that I could do the same. This is simply my faith, combining with the faith of the other person, that allows us to access heaven. As I shared before, the first time I went to heaven, I had an addiction to prostitutes, and I think that is important for you to consider if you think that you are not worthy to go to heaven yourself.

God loves his people. Wouldn't your life be wonderful if you came to a place where you could access heaven any time that you felt you wanted to visit? We are seated in heavenly places, so all we really need to do is to open our eyes to see it.

Chapter 8

Drinking a Pina Colada

As I shared before in an earlier chapter, I was often going about my business and taking care of my responsibilities on earth when I'd suddenly appear in heaven in my mind. It's unmistakable.

When you're appearing in a different place in heaven, you start to see images or pictures from heaven in your mind. You can't dismiss them. You might think it's just your imagination, but if you are spiritually in tune, you will realize where you are.

You can start to engage. Start to concentrate with your imagination. Concentrate on what you can see in your mind, and if there are people in the vision, start to interact with them. Start to talk to them and listen in your spirit as Jesus speaks to your spirit. Listen to what they have to say.

If you meet someone, listen for a name in your spirit, such as Joseph or Michael or John or Moses. Talk to the saints, interact with them, try and find out why you're there and really press into the encounter.

During one encounter, I was in bed. Every night before I go to sleep, I talk to Jesus back and forth in conversations. I ask him questions, and he answers me. I talk about my day and what I've been through that day. He'll discuss it with me, and we have this debriefing session after each day.

I was talking to Jesus, and I suddenly appeared on a wooden deck in my imagination. Jesus was there. We were sitting in two arm chairs on this wooden deck, and Jesus handed me a drink. He said, "Here's a drink, have a drink." I heard in my head, "Pina colada." That's how I hear things in heaven and how I hear things in the spirit.

I recognized that "Pina colada" was the name of a popular cocktail drink. At the time, I didn't know what a Pina colada was made of. As I was talking to Jesus and discussing life with him as we sat on this back deck, overlooking the Crystal Sea, I was sipping this drink, and on earth, I could taste pineapple in my mouth.

The flavor of pineapple was infusing my mouth. A Pina colada is made out of Malibu rum, which is a coconut rum and pineapple juice. Well, Malibu rum is one of my favorite rums. I used to drink Malibu rum in milk and Malibu rum in Coca-Cola, so it was one of my favorite drinks.

When I had the Pina colada with Jesus in heaven, it proved to me that there's alcohol in heaven. At the time, I was worshiping at a Salvation Army Church, serving as a Salvation Army soldier. That meant that I couldn't drink alcohol when I was in uniform for the Salvation Army. The Salvation Army has instituted the rule that if you're a soldier in uniform, you don't drink alcohol as a witness to other people.

This is not really a religious matter. It's a set of rules for Salvation Army people who go into hotels and pubs so that they can be a witness to people without consuming alcohol. In this way, former alcoholics could become part of the Salvation Army Church and witness in hotels and pubs without being forced to drink. People usually know that Salvation Army officers don't drink when they're in uniform. The uniform served as protection for ex-alcoholics.

Since I was a soldier in uniform at the time, I think Jesus respected the fact that I wasn't drinking. The alcohol taste in the Pina colada didn't come through to me in earth, so all I tasted was pineapple, but I didn't taste the rum. Believe me, if it happened now, I would taste the rum since I don't belong to the Salvation Army anymore. I really enjoy having an alcoholic Pina colada, and I've had them since this happened.

Here I was in heaven, overlooking the Crystal Sea, and I had this wonderful encounter with Jesus. Rather than debriefing in my bed while looking at the ceiling, I instead had a view of the Crystal Sea in heaven.

I was talking to Jesus and had this beautiful view with a breeze blowing. We were on recliners with chairs that leaned back. This was a really beautiful and unexpected encounter. Like I've said, you might find that some of your early encounters with heaven were not initiated by you but were initiated by heaven. When you have them, it's totally surprising and enjoyable and really memorable for you. Again, this happened to me when I first began having my encounters with heaven.

I hope that you enjoyed this explanation of heaven. I hope that you're able to see what I've described.

Lessons Learned

One thing I learned from this encounter is that Jesus is aware of your preferences and your likes. I have since ordered a Pina colada and enjoyed drinking it. I find it so sweet and thoughtful that Jesus chose a drink for me with coconut rum, which is one of my favorite drinks.

Another thing I learned was that Jesus would love for us to come to heaven and interact with him rather than for us to stay on earth. I have since visited my mansion in heaven and recognized this decking overlooking the Crystal Sea to actually be the view from the second story of my mansion.

I find it so comforting that Jesus would summon me to heaven and enjoy my favorite drink with me as we chatted about what was happening in my life. I am sure that as I write this, that Jesus would like all of us to come and visit him in heaven as often as we want.

Chapter 9

Great Cloud of Witnesses Speak

I've been through a lot of pain and suffering for many years of my life. With so many struggles, my life hasn't been too enjoyable. After a few encounters, Jesus told me that he really misses me and that I'm welcome to come to heaven anytime that I choose.

However, I found that my encounters with heaven sometimes left me sad. As a result, I hesitated to go to heaven simply because of the letdown when I returned. The presence of God is so strong there with a feeling of bliss. Since heaven is such a beautiful place and since it's so enjoyable to spend time there in the presence of God, coming back to earth is really a jolt. One way to explain it is that when people get high on drugs, they enjoy an amazing high, but after the high, they come down off the drug and crash.

Sadly, the same can be true of experiencing heaven. It's a shock and a jolt to come back to earth and all of the pain and the realities that we face. Even if you had the ability and an open invitation to go to heaven, you might not want to go regularly because it can be difficult to come back to earth.

Many people don't understand that. They say, "Well, if God allowed me to go to heaven, I'd go all the time." That might be true of you. You might be able to handle it without any problem because you don't live a life like I've lived or have such struggles on earth.

I wrote a book about my visits to heaven called, "Great Cloud of Witnesses Speak." In that book, I interviewed 19 saints from heaven. I put together 10 standard questions for each of the saints and asked each of them these questions. I added a couple of extra questions based on the saint's life.

One of the questions is, "What do you like about heaven?" As the saints answered that question, I had a vision of heaven. When you add up all of the descriptions of heaven from each of the 19 saints, it's equal to 30 or 40 pages of information in the book.

I really encourage you to buy "Great Cloud of Witnesses Speak" and go through each of their answers because they really explain heaven in an amazing way with a lot of depth and understanding about how heaven operates.

As I was interviewing the saints and as they were answering my questions about heaven, I was sitting in my family room. As I explained heaven, I was caught up in a vision to heaven and witnessed what they were discussing. As they each explained heaven, I could see heaven as they described it, just like in this book. They told about certain scenes in heaven. If you read the book, you can be there, and you can experience those scenes with me.

Rahab, in the book, "Great Cloud of Witnesses Speak," talks about her restaurants in heaven. She has three signature restaurants in heaven, and she shares how the people of heaven come to her restaurants where she cooks meals.

As she explained her restaurants in heaven, I was able to experience the restaurants and actually see them and watch her serving food as she interacted with the customers there.

Jesus really used the interviews in those books so that I would encounter heaven and see it and be used to go there. Jesus knows that my life will be a whole lot richer when I'm used to going to heaven. Essentially, this book is just a collection of simple stories and simple encounters with heaven. If I have more encounters with heaven, I will write more books about them in the future.

Lessons Learned

What I learned from my encounters with the 19 saints and their description of what they liked about heaven is that everyone encounters something different in heaven. To some people, the throne room is their favorite part, yet others might enjoy the people of heaven and the love that exists between them. Everyone who goes to heaven will be delighted. Heaven will seem as if it is perfectly designed for you when you arrive.

I learned that God wanted me to experience heaven, and he would use whatever means he could to get me there. I was surprised as each saint described to me what they liked about heaven. I could see their individual personalities through their descriptions.

I know that I will not only benefit from my travels to heaven, but it is my prayer that I will learn to encounter heaven more often.

Chapter 10

Seeing a Ballerina Dance a Solo

Sometimes, when I'm describing a scene in heaven, I see just what I am saying. For instance, I might see everything that I describe to the other person as I hold someone's hand or talk to them on Skype and take them on a visitation of heaven and go through the fountain experience with the walking lion and the lamb and the children. As I experience a vision in heaven and as I explain it to someone else, they encounter it as well.

Even on the other side of the world, I see what I'm describing as we go into a mansion, a building or the throne room. In this way, I confirm to them that they're seeing the same thing. I can tell them what they're seeing in their spirit at the same time.

We hold hands in the spirit and go to the same place. The Holy Spirit grabs my spirit and their spirit and takes us to the heavenlies, and we're able to encounter the same thing. This dynamic—impossible to do logically—is completely possible with the help of the Holy Spirit, the Spirit of God. God is able to do the impossible.

One time, I was giving a girl a prophecy, and I told her that she wanted to be a ballerina from a young age but that the desire and the heart was taken from her because of certain circumstances. Even so, it had remained as a really emotional desire in her heart, and she had wished all her life that she could be a ballerina. In the prophecy, Jesus said that he wants her to know that when she's in heaven, she'll be trained as a ballerina and she will dance there.

As I wrote the prophecy, I saw a vision of this troop of ballerinas coming out to dance on the stage in the throne room, and the whole of the throne room of heaven was watching. This troop came out, and then, a ballerina came to the front. She performed the solo, and the troop stepped back. She came down the hundred stairs that separate the floor of the throne room from the thrones. She was performing a beautiful solo dance on the platform between the congregation and the stairs.

As I was typing up the prophecy and sharing what this woman was going to do one day in the throne room, my eyes started to fill with tears. I was emotionally really affected by giving her the prophecy. I kept on typing and wiped away my tears to finish the prophecy and sent it off to her.

After I sent her the prophecy, I wondered why I was so emotionally affected. Jesus told me that the ballerina that I saw in the vision was actually a real ballerina doing a solo. I wasn't actually seeing someone in the future but was watching a live dance by a ballerina in the throne room as a high command performance in front of God, his angels and the saints of heaven. This was very special as a key event in heaven as she danced in the throne room in front of everyone.

49

Jesus told me that the ballerina that I was watching was my sister. My mother had a stillborn baby, and I was crying as I watched her dance. My sister, Karen, was the ballerina and is still alive in heaven.

I was watching her perform live when I gave the prophecy, which moved me emotionally and brought me to tears. She is a star ballerina, an excellent dancer. She gave a real command performance.

This vision deeply affected me. Since I've met my sister in heaven and had her visit me here, I've come to know her well. I also have another sister in heaven, Talitha, who died when my mom had a miscarriage.

Talitha and I have grown very close. She is a painter with an art gallery. I've been there, and I share her story in the next chapter.

Karen is also friends with Mary Magdalene, who is a heavenly mentor to me. I have met her a couple of hundred times on earth and visited her in heaven. Through these visits, we've spent a lot of time together.

Mary is also a dancer and a ballerina as well as a worshipper in heaven. She knows Karen, my sister, really well. Since Mary was going to have a big impact in my life and teach me a lot of lessons, she grew close to both of my sisters in heaven and developed a good friendship and relationship with them.

I hope that you're encouraged by that. One lesson that you can take out of this is that everyone has a purpose in heaven. As I mentioned in a previous chapter, Rahab is a chef in heaven. Karen, my sister, is a ballerina who worships, dances and holds performances for people in heaven. They can attend the ballet in heaven and watch ballerinas dance.

My sister, Talitha, is an artist, and people collect her artwork. Our lesson from this is that people do all kinds of jobs and have different purposes in heaven. Heaven is not just a place for you to go and spend all your time in the throne room, worshipping God. You can actually work and serve him and others there in a more complete and deeper way.

Lessons Learned

I was so comforted to know that all stillborn babies, every miscarriage or every abortion, and any child that dies when they are young, goes to heaven. I loved meeting my sister this way while she danced a solo in heaven. I was overcome with tears as I watched her. I didn't find out that she was my sister until after I finished the prophecy.

Everyone has a purpose in heaven. We don't spend all our time worshipping God in the throne room. We all have jobs to do that we love. You will be busy doing what you have always wanted to do when you are in heaven. Rahab also writes fiction in heaven, and many people there read her books. When they meet her, they suggest new books for her to write.

If you have a restaurant in heaven, you don't have to pay for advertising but as you change your menus, the new menus are delivered to everyone that wants to visit your restaurant. As a ballerina, Karen performs many different ballets, and people also receive flyers delivered to their mansion if they are interested in ballet. Everyone in heaven does fun activities and helps other people.

You might be interested in the fact that no one holds menial jobs in heaven, such as washing dishes or garbage collecting. These things are done though the miracle of heaven.

Chapter 11

An Artist in Heaven

In the last chapter, we encountered my older sister who was the stillborn baby of my mother. Her death really upset my mother. After the stillborn baby, my mother had a miscarriage. Finally, she had my sister, Carmen.

I came to realize that the miscarriage was Talitha. During my recording of the "Great Cloud of Witnesses," Mary Magdalene came down from heaven with Talitha. When she arrived for her interview, Talitha was named after the word that Jesus called to the little girl when he brought her back from the dead in Mark 5:41.

After the visits to heaven, I've come to know Talitha. She is an artist, and I don't know a lot about art, but she paints a lot of still life paintings of people, portraits and scenes with people in them. She also paints landscapes and can do abstract paintings. She has a gallery in heaven, which is five stories high.

The first three stories of the gallery are paintings that she has painted of scenes and people in heaven. The fourth story in the gallery is scenes from the lives of my mother, father, sisters and brothers. And the fifth story of her gallery in heaven is scenes from my life.

Since I have a great calling on my life and since I'm pretty important to the people in heaven, and they love to go up to the fifth story and watch the scenes of my life. Certain paintings in heaven are interactive so that when you approach the painting, it comes alive and plays a video.

Talitha has paintings of me surfing. When you go up to the painting of me surfing, the wave will start before the picture and then continue with me riding my surfboard in the wave until we come to the point of where the picture is, and then, the video will continue to the end of the wave. The picture becomes this video that plays a very lifelike scene from my past.

So you can go through the fifth story of that gallery and look at the paintings and the special events of my life. It's really encouraging.

Talitha is one of the many artists in heaven. Artists in heaven paint. Everyone in heaven has a job and has something to do. In heaven, there's no income or wages. You actually do your job for the love of what you do.

When you paint paintings in heaven, people can come and secure the paintings without paying anything for them. They can just take the painting for their mansion or for a relative's mansion that's just about to die and come to heaven.

Talitha continues to paint paintings for the first four stories of her gallery. She also continues to paint paintings from my life as it progresses in the fifth story.

In my recent trip to heaven, saints met me, and I interviewed them. Their interviews were recorded. Any saint who had their interview recorded by me can take a painting of me to hang in their mansion. I've been told through prophetic words and through Jesus and as the Holy Spirit moved on other people that I'm pretty important in heaven.

The people of heaven really love me, and they really want paintings of me. They enjoy being interviewed. I certainly enjoy people on earth hearing what they have to say. The interviews are excellent and entertaining as well. Talitha is happy and fulfilled. She really loves watching my life.

I want to share something else about heaven because we have some time in this chapter and some space to fill. In heaven, they have movies, like a drive-in theater screen. On the screen, people watch the saints' lives play. They will play my whole past. Anyone can go and watch my entire life—my past, my future and everything that I will achieve.

Any saint in heaven that interacts with you as part of your great cloud of witnesses, part of the people that will influence your life, will watch everything you've suffered and everything you've been through in your whole life on those screens. They can get to the point where they're watching your future on this big screen in heaven like a drive-in theatre. Thousands of people can watch your life at once. They then make decrees over your life and pray over you so that what they see for the future comes to pass.

Talitha and Mary Magdalene and other saints that interact with me have watched my whole future. They've watched my sufferings and everything that I will achieve.

They have seen this book. They have seen it edited. They have seen it typed up. They have seen the finished product. They have seen the cover and have seen people buying it.

At this moment, if you are open to it, you can imagine the people of heaven actually watching you read this book right now. Just as you read this book or listen to it on audio, the people of heaven are watching you.

Lessons Learned

I first saw my house in heaven and noticed that the pictures/tapestries on my wall came alive when I went close to them. I later read the same thing in a book by Kat Kerr, "Revealing Heaven"—pictures in heaven come alive when you look at them. I am not sure if what Kat said influenced me, but the first time I looked at some of the paintings that Talitha painted of me, I saw them turn into a video.

Heaven has many things and places to encounter. God, through the Holy Spirit, knows what you need to see. If you visit heaven, there will be a reason why you see each of the things that you see.

It means so much to me that much of my life is being captured in paintings by my sister. I am not a person who has many photos of my life. I must have known in my spirit that heaven was recording my life.

Talitha, my sister, is not the only artist to paint scenes from my life. In the future, 10 to 20 years from now, many people in the world will know me, and I will be a lot more popular if I am to believe the prophetic words that have been spoken over my life. Some people might question my writing or feel I have a big ego writing this, but I have to share that it is humbling to me to write this.

The enemy is constantly telling me that this book is no good and not informative, but it is my hope that this book will encourage you to go and have your own adventures in heaven. Your visits to heaven, not mine, will mean the most to you.

Chapter 12

My Mansion

After numerous visits to heaven, I then went through a process of nine visits to heaven to show me my mansion there. Some people have a simple house in heaven because that's all they ever wanted. Others have a house in the forest or even a tree house. Other folks just want a basic farm house. Still others are given mansions. I initially thought that my house was just a small house and not a mansion.

Income and material possessions have never been important to me. I don't own the best clothes or even a car. I don't own many possessions, and money doesn't mean much to me, so only God in his wisdom has decided that I'll have a mansion when I go to heaven.

You can enter my mansion through a couple of pillars and two open doors. When you come into my mansion on the right-hand side, you see a commercial kitchen. If you've seen a kitchen in a restaurant with benches around the sides, it's similar to that with two rows of benches. It's full of equipment. The kitchen could cater for a restaurant with 200 people and serve a la carte meals on demand.

If you come out of the kitchen, you enter what Americans might call the "family room." Two of the walls have a tapestry. One of the tapestries has Mary Magdalene washing Jesus' feet with her tears and an alabaster jar of perfume. She was the woman who came to the Pharisee's house and washed Jesus' feet with her tears in the Gospels.

Once you go up close to the scene, it becomes a portal, and you can actually go to Mary Magdalene's house. If you walk through the tapestry, you'll end up in Mary Magdalene's house.

For many years, I felt that I had an assignment from God. I was very obedient, and I used to tell God that the only reward I wanted was to be able to live next to Mary Magdalene in heaven. She was a friend of mine. It turns out that her house is not next to mine in heaven. Instead, I have a doorway/portal in my house that leads to her house.

On another wall hangs a tapestry of the Lion of the Tribe of Judah, which is a manifestation of Jesus. A group of children surround the lion. If you walk up to that picture, the lion comes alive, and it becomes a portal into the children's playground where some of the aborted children play. These children are very important to me.

All through the walls of the house is a 2-feet-high aquarium with fish swimming in it. One of the fish is named Harry. Harry has prophesied to me and spoken to me before. All the animals in heaven speak from spirit to spirit. In the future, my favorite cat will live there as will all my cats from my childhood. All your pets go to heaven, so it's a misunderstanding that pets don't have a spirit and that they don't go to heaven.

If you go upstairs, you will see a long and winding staircase to the second level. A 150-feet heated swimming pool is on the next level at the top of the stairs. I will enjoy swimming laps in it and hosting big pool parties.

A 50-seat coffee shop with two coffee machines and baristas who make the coffee is past the swimming pool. Another kitchen is behind the coffee shop that serves meals, so the café is fully catered. Fifty seats are inside with 20 more seats outside. The picture on the cover of this book represents the type of coffee shop you might have in your mansion.

Outside is the balcony where Jesus and I drank the Pina colada. Looking out over the balcony, you can see the Crystal Sea and a wharf with a yacht moored to it that I will own. The yacht sleeps eight people although in heaven, you don't sleep.

I've visited the coffee shop many times with my friend who has gone to heaven with me.

Past the coffee shop is a movie theatre that seats 80 to 100 people. It shows both films that were made on earth and films that were made in heaven. I love films and find them so inspiring. I once heard that Steven Spielberg had a cinema in his house, and I wished I had a house with one. Jesus must have heard my thought.

That is one thig about your house. The commercial kitchen in my house was a secret desire of mine. Like I said, I wanted to live next to Mary. I once saw a saltwater aquarium in my cousin's house, so God put one through all of the walls in my house. The fish follow me from room to room. Everything that you have ever desired if you had enough money on earth will be in your house in heaven.

If you go further past the movie cinema in my house, you will see an office on the right with staff, a television studio, computers and a radio studio. In heaven, I will lecture, write, produce films and TV shows and more. In heaven, I will teach on the things of God. Further down the hall is a library with all the books that I will have read by the time I am in heaven. This includes all the books that I want to read and all the books that I will have written before then.

Just considering the second story with a 150-feet pool, a café, a theater, a professional film studio, a radio studio, an office and a library, I have a large mansion.

I have not yet seen the third story of my house, but I know that many people will come and spend time there. I wouldn't have a 50-seat café and a commercial kitchen and a movie cinema that seats 100 people if I weren't going to entertain. Perhaps you can come to my house for a meal and a movie.

Lessons Learned

The first thing I learned about God when I managed to see a bit of my house was that God must listen to our secret wishes. I used to go to a club to exercise and listen to music there. They had a coffee shop that I loved, and I thought to myself that if I were ever rich, I would have one in my own house. Each part of my house in heaven has been made up of these secret desires that I have had throughout life.

I know when you get to heaven and you see your house, you won't see anything that is unfamiliar to you. Your mansion will have your favorite things. Everything you could desire will be there.

Going to my house in heaven showed me just how invested God is in my life. Thoughts that I had 25 years ago have been saved and that wish was then put in my house. God really does love us more than we can consider. I know that many people know me on social media and would love to meet me, and I know through prophecies that I have had over my life that many people in the world will know me before I die, so I understand how my house needs to be large enough to entertain many people in heaven.

If you have the opportunity to go to heaven and have a look at your house, you will see it decorated and made up of features that you have always desired. You might come to realize that God knows you and your life much better than you previously thought. Seeing your house in heaven will energize you and make you draw closer to Jesus on earth.

As a person that has been to heaven a number of times, I have come to realize that heaven is so much better than earth. With no disease, no sin and no suffering, you will really enjoy heaven.

Chapter 13

Popular Engineer and CEO in Heaven

I have stressed that part of a mature and supernatural Christian life involves obedience. I could have kept out the information about my addiction to prostitutes in this book. However, the Holy Spirit, in his wisdom, chose for me to keep it in to show you that you don't have to overcome sin to go to heaven. God's grace is unbelievable, and Jesus' blood is enough. Even if you are still practicing sin and if you haven't conquered that sin in your life, you can still go to heaven.

I have since conquered my addiction to prostitutes. I could have withheld that information from this book. I could've not written "The Great Cloud of Witnesses Speak" because people might accuse me of necromancy and say that I'm speaking with the dead and that it's not biblical.

Jesus himself spoke to Moses and Elijah on the Mount of Transfiguration, so if speaking to the dead wasn't allowed even through the Holy Spirit's guidance, then Jesus would have been in sin by speaking to people that had passed on. I could have left out the chapter that mentions a great cloud of witnesses, but I included it. I could've left out the fact that I've met saints on earth, including Mary Magdalene and my sisters. Saints from heaven have come down and visited with me. Leaving out all of these things might have stopped people from complaining and having an issue with this book.

But everything comes down to obedience. Jesus is the one who chooses what I will talk about in each book. He's the one who decides what subjects I will address, and through the Holy Spirit, he chooses what I will say and share in this book. And so, I say all this as an introduction to what follows.

I personally believe that the following person I talk about had an encounter with Jesus on his deathbed and gave his life to Jesus. His sister wrote an article about how he regained consciousness on his death bed. As he awoke, he was exclaiming, "Wow, wow, wow!"

I've met Steve Jobs, the founder of Apple, on a number of occasions after his death. I've even interviewed him, but I didn't publish the interview. In the midst of interviewing Steve Jobs, I asked him what his house was like in heaven, and he told me about it. As I was interviewing him and listening to his explanation, I could see the house as he described it. I saw his family room where you normally watch TV with chairs and sofas there.

Steve has an open ceiling and a 100-foot waterfall coming down off a rock ledge in that room. This waterfall is falling into a lake of water in his house. You can sit on one of his sofas and talk to him, and a waterfall is just 30 feet from you.

It is so peaceful and beautiful. It doesn't matter that his roof is open because it doesn't rain in heaven that I know of except in selected places. I'm told that rain won't come through the roof.

The water from the waterfall is piped somewhere else; otherwise, the whole house would flood. The house is just beautiful and has a lot of sapphire in it with a lot of blue.

I've also seen his office buildings and seen him with hundreds of engineers. Like I shared before with you, you discern things in heaven according to what you understand and your theologies and your doctrines on earth. Ten people might see the throne room, and they can each see different things according to what they believe.

I've seen his office with 100 engineers. They are in a room with many computers, designing software, programs and technology for earth. The engineers and software and product designers on earth will receive ideas and downloads from these engineers in heaven. Steve Jobs is overseeing engineers in heaven who are designing, implementing and creating technology there. The creators on earth are receiving downloads into their minds from heaven from what Steve Jobs is creating.

This applies to Google, Facebook, YouTube and other similar platforms that we don't even know about yet. Steve Jobs had an encounter with heaven; he had a vision of heaven and met Jesus while he was unconscious as he was dying.

Steve Jobs is in heaven, and I've met him. On earth, when I talked to him after his death, he talked about how heaven has changed him and how he had some rough edges in his personality when he was on earth. He's different now, and he has a beautiful house and a workplace in heaven where he's very busy doing the things that he was created to do. He's passed on from earth with all his abilities and his driven personality that is all about innovation and creativity and excellence. Now, he's working in heaven creating things, designing things for heaven and designing things for earth.

Lessons Learned

The biggest lesson that I learned from meeting Steve Jobs is that God is in control of the destiny of people and where they end up. Steve possibly had thousands of Christians who loved him and who were praying for him. I am always happy to hear that Jesus is able to save people on their deathbed and take them to heaven.

Some people might mock me and say that I have no proof that Steve is in heaven. I guess those people will have to wait till they go to heaven to prove that I am wrong. I always remember the thief on the cross who was saved just before Jesus died. When someone is saved, many church people think that they need to prove it first. They want to see mature fruit before they believe that a person is a Christian.

This account should encourage anyone who is praying for a family member or a friend that currently doesn't know the Lord. God is quite able to save people right at the last minute.

I don't mind people thinking that I am in error or that I have been deceived with a false vision. That is their right. I am compelled to include this chapter in the book because I know this will bring hope to many people about loved ones they are praying for.

Chapter 14

Being in Heaven without my Knowledge

Throughout the course of this book, I've shared with you that I've had a hard life. I was told that I could go to heaven as often as I wish and that I can visit heaven anytime I like. God likes to encourage me to go to heaven because it builds my faith and the faith of others when I share it.

Throughout my life, I went through much a lot of pain and suffering. I share my story in my book, "His Redeeming Love: A Memoir," which tells of my life up until 2014. I encourage you to buy this book so that you can read about how I have lived and how that helped me become the person that I am today. I want you to understand as you read this book that I'm no one special. I'm not a super Christian or someone who's out of touch with the ordinary Christian.

My encounters and experiences in heaven are true for me, but they can also be true for you. You can reach a stage of obedience and faith and have a teachable spirit so that you also encounter heaven. I could take you to heaven on a visitation where you can become used to the portal and start to access heaven for yourself anytime you like. You could start to have experiences in heaven and interact with heaven. If you have enough encounters, you can write your own book about them.

For many years, I lived with emotional pain. I'd be walking somewhere through the city in a lot of pain and with a lot of sadness. Then, all of a sudden, I'd feel joy; I'd feel peace, and I'd feel love. My whole frame of mind, my whole mood, would dramatically change from darkness to light.

At the same time, a song might play that would encourage me. However, many times, I just couldn't put my finger on it. I'd just be walking along through the city of Sydney, feeling down, rejected, sad, depressed and hurting inside. All of sudden, I'd feel joy, peace, love and comfort. I never knew why.

Eventually, Jesus told me that he'd often take me to heaven when I was down. I'd actually be walking through Sydney and through the atmosphere of heaven, and I'd be in two places at once. I'd be on earth and in heaven at the same time.

Recently, I was talking to a good friend of mine on Skype. She read my book, "Great Cloud of Witnesses Speak," and she wrote to me as the author and said that she really wanted to get to know me and become my friend. We now talk a lot on Skype.

She heard from the Holy Spirit, and once, she told me, "You've been to heaven many times but have not been aware of it."

I agreed. "That's true. I have, and Jesus used to take me to heaven a lot. I didn't know that I was in heaven, but I just suddenly felt good and felt happy. God was taking me to heaven to cheer me up." This could have happened to you also.

You might have visited heaven already. Have you ever been really dejected, sad and depressed and then all of a sudden, felt joy, peace and confidence? Have you ever had a turnaround in your emotions, but you did not know why? Perhaps you have been to heaven, too!

Lessons Learned

For many years, I was encountering heaven without knowing it or having any memory of it. God is so faithful. Imagine God thinking up a way to bring great feelings to his people. Imagine that he would bring their spirits to heaven if they became too sad so that they could encounter the atmosphere there.

I can only thank God for this. We serve such a loving and considerate God. To think that he loved me so much that he had a quick fix for my sadness. He just took it upon himself to allow me to be in heaven even without my knowledge. When my friend told me this, she really didn't understand what she was saying. When I was able to share what had happened to me, then she understood.

I have to thank God for these experiences. It is my prayer that he does this for many of the readers of this book when they feel down and upset.

Chapter 15

My Visits to the Galactic Council

As I've shared a couple of times already in the book, Jesus wanted me to go to heaven and to experience it. I have an open invitation to heaven. Many of you who have heard about my visits might have thought to yourself, "If I were invited to heaven, I'd go every time. I'd spend all my time there."

I know that some of you don't relate to the painful life that I have lived. You don't really understand why coming back to earth is so hard for me. But some of you can now relate to the fact that even though heaven is awesome and a wonderful place to visit, coming back to earth might be difficult.

Jesus circumvented that when he had me do the interviews with the great cloud of witnesses. Every time they talked about heaven, I went there again. Not only is the question about what they like about heaven very interesting, but the saints give some really insightful answers to the questions that I asked. That is another example of a time when the Lord took me to heaven. This was not against my will, but he used something I was doing to take me to there.

Another time that I went to heaven was when I was working on my book, "My Visits to the Galactic Council of Heaven." By the time you read this book, I will have published that book as well. In that book, a prophet that lived on earth came down and visited with me and started mentoring me. Then, he started to take me to a council in heaven made up of 11 saints and Jesus. I went to this place, and the saints talked to me and encouraged me and shared on different topics with me. I visited part of an arena with 10,000 people from heaven in it. Sometimes, people from the audience of 10,000 people in heaven come down and talk to me.

I am working on this series of books called "My Visits to the Galactic Council of Heaven." I will be writing book 1, book 2, book 3, etc. I will continue to release books in this series so that every time I go to this place with the galactic council, I'm going to heaven.

Jesus has arranged it so that I go to heaven quite often. I interact with saints like John the Apostle, Bob Jones, John Paul Jackson, John the Baptist, Malachi, Elijah, Enoch and more. By the time this book comes out, the other book will have been published, so you might want to check it out.

I've been on visits to the galactic council room in heaven and the arena that is part of it. I have to say that the atmosphere is completely different from the atmosphere found on earth. There's no judging, no evil, no jealousy. There's nothing but love and encouragement and edification. If you go there and if you're feeling depressed, you come out of there feeling uplifted and alive and free from your depression. It is just an amazing place. I really encourage you to get to a place with the Lord where you can visit and encounter heaven.

Before I finish, I also want to mention Kat Kerr, an author. She has two books on heaven, available in paperback, called "Revealing Heaven," available in Part 1 and Part 2. The books have some exciting stories about heaven. She also has a lot of videos on YouTube that explain heaven and her encounters with heaven.

In her books, she explains that heaven has theme parks where you can go and ride on roller coasters, and you can buy hot dogs and cotton candy. You can play games similar to what you play at a fair. Heaven has a movie theater, and films are made there. Everyone has a job there. Heaven has many amazing things.

Even though I have been to heaven a number of times, I certainly haven't seen much there. However, I've been to the Crystal Sea. My house actually backs up to it with a really great view of it off the deck of my house on the second floor. I expect that I'll have many more encounters with heaven. In the future, I might write another book of these encounters.

I hope that you've really enjoyed this book, and I hope that you can have your own encounters of heaven, too.

Lessons Learned

I guess the reason that Jesus arranged for me to visit the galactic council in heaven is that he wants me to learn from some of his saints. He wants the readers of the books to be blessed from reading them as well. Some things that God has us do are beyond our understanding. I enjoy going and visiting the galactic council whenever I go. I really enjoy the atmosphere of heaven when I am there. As I write more books, I hope that people will be able to visit their own council of saints in the future.

Closing Thoughts

Many of you who bought this book on Kindle will be glad that it was only 99 cents. Some of you might be sad that you did not see enough of heaven in this book. What I can tell you is that one encounter by yourself with your own visit will be better than any encounters that you read about in books.

However, many people read encounters in books and actually see the encounter in their spirits and can enter through a portal into their own encounter in the same place. Many times, I have been reading the Gospels and have had a vision when I read the accounts and have gone back in time to the actual event. I have walked and talked with Jesus 2,000 years ago.

One great way to start to have encounters is to read other people's encounters and focus your mind and enter into the encounter. When you can see yourself in the same place, you can start to have your own encounter. You can read of other people's accounts in heaven in the Bible and focus on those accounts until they open up heaven for you.

Many of the things that we are hungry for we actually receive. God creates a desire in us, a hunger in us, for a reason. When you have read some books on heaven, and you have a real hunger to visit, feel free to contact me through my website. Give me a donation that you think is fair, and I will take you to heaven.

It is my hope that you have gotten your money's worth whether you purchased a paperback, bought the e-book or listened to this on Audible.

Please remember that one day in the courts of the Lord is better than a thousand elsewhere. I pray that you experience your own "one day" soon.

God bless you.

I'd love to hear from you

One of the ways that you can bless me as a writer is by writing an honest and candid review of my book on Amazon. I always read the reviews of my books, and I would love to hear what you have to say about this one.

Before I buy a book, I read the reviews first. You can make an informed decision about a book when you have read enough honest reviews from readers. One way to help me sell this book and to give me positive feedback is by writing a review for me. It doesn't cost you a thing but helps me and the future readers of this book enormously.

If you would like to sow money into my book writing ministry like the person who financed this book did or if you would like to sow a portion of money into a book, please visit my website and ask me what projects I am working on.

To read my blog or to request a life coaching session or your own personal prophecy from God, you can also visit my website at http://personal-prophecy-today.com. All of your gifts will go toward the books that I write and self-publish. You can also visit my website to request your own visit to heaven.

To write to me about this book or any other thoughts that you have, please feel free to contact me at my personal email address at survivors.sanctuary@gmail.com.

You can also friend request me on Facebook at Matthew Robert Payne. Please send me a message if we have no friends in common as a lot of scammers now send me friend requests.

You can also do me a huge favor and share this book on Facebook as a recommended book to read. This will help me and other readers.

Other Books by Matthew Robert Payne

The Parables of Jesus Made Simple

The Prophetic Supernatural Experience

Prophetic Evangelism Made Simple

Your Identity in Christ

His Redeeming Love- A Memoir

Writing and Self-Publishing Christian Nonfiction

Coping with your Pain and Suffering

Living for Eternity

Jesus Speaking Today

Great Cloud of Witnesses Speak

My Radical Encounters with Angels

Finding Intimacy with Jesus Made Simple

My Radical Encounters with Angels- Book Two

A Beginner's Guide to the Prophetic

Michael Jackson Speaks from Heaven

7 Keys to Intimacy with Jesus

Conversations with God Book 1

Optimistic Visions of Revelation

Conversations with God Book 2

Finding Your Purpose in Christ

Influencing your World for Christ: Practical Everyday Evangelism

My Visits to the Galactic Council of Heaven

You can find my published books on my Amazon author page here:
http://tinyurl.com/jq3h893

Upcoming Books:

Deep Calls unto Deep: Answering Questions about the Prophetic

Great Cloud of Witnesses Speak: Old and New

5 Key Verses that Will Transform Your Life

About the Author

Matthew was raised in a Baptist church and was led to the Lord at the tender age of 8. He has experienced some pain and darkness in his life, which has given him a deep compassion and love for all people.

Today, he runs two Facebook groups, one called "Open Heavens and Intimacy with Jesus" and one called "Prophetic Training Group." Matthew has a commission from the Lord to train up prophets and to mentor others in the Christian faith. He does this through his groups and by writing relevant books for the Christian faith.

God has commissioned him to write at least 50 books in his life, and he spends his days writing and earning the money to self-publish. You can support him by donating money at http://personal-prophecy-today.com or by requesting your own personal prophecy, life-coaching session or visit to heaven.

It is Matthew's prayer that this book has blessed you, and he hopes it will lead you into a deeper and more intimate relationship with God.

CPSIA information can be obtained
at www.ICGtesting.com
Printed in the USA
BVOW06s1817190417
481724BV00015B/129/P